Xchange

Micro Makes

Michael Cox
and Jo Cox

A colourful collection of fun things to make, grow and cook. Plus some Interesting Info, Frenetic Funnies and Dippy Data!

Almost everyone's got the urge to create – it could be an ocean-going liner or a ship in a bottle, a scrumptious banquet or a dog's dinner – the list's endless! But there's no doubt about it, making things is satisfying, challenging, rewarding ... and loads of fun!

Contents

Smiley sunflower faces	2	Beanie baby	16
Fruit squelch	3	Sexton Blake . . . fake!	18
A cuddly vampire bat sock puppet	4	A gorgeous garden lantern	20
Chocolate chip vanilla cookies	6	Images with impact	21
Feisty face lifts	8	Something 'buzzy'!	22
Create a fabulous widescreen 'photorama'	10	Shear magic – a topiary bird	24
Make your own marvellous miniature garden paradise	12	Fiercesome flapping vampire	26
		Groovy garlic bread	28
Scrummy spud and bacon cakes	14	Send garden birds nuts!	29
Say it with flowers	15	Brilliant beaded bracelet	30
		Minute mouth-watering mini pizzas	32

Published by BBC Educational Publishing, BBC White City, 201 Wood Lane, London W12 7TS.
First published 2001
© Michael Cox/BBC Worldwide (Educational Publishing), 2001
Reproduction by Spectrum Printed in Italy by Poligrafico Dehoniano

All rights reserved. No part of this publication may be reproduced, stored in any form or by any means mechanical, electronic, recording or otherwise without prior permission of the publisher.
ISBN 0 563 54390 6

Smiley sunflower faces

This will brighten up the dullest days, peskiest people and gloomiest gardens. Sunflowers are those enormous yellow things that the famous Dutch artist Vincent van Gogh was forever painting. Their seeds are used to make sunflower oil and margarine. In some places they're used to make bread and feed hens. They grow in huge quantities in fields in France but are also grown in Britain in gardens and a few fields too. Here's how to bring a smile to their faces!

what you need

- Some sunflower seeds
- Some plant pots
- Potting compost

What you do

1. Plant your seeds (spring is the best time). Follow the instructions on the seed packet. Starting them off indoors in pots will give them a flying start.
2. Once your sunflowers look strong and healthy, and are about 30cm high, transplant them to a warm, sunny spot in your garden.
3. Be kind to your sunflowers – so feed them, water them and talk to them (but don't take them for walks).
4. You will need to tie them to a strong, tall cane when they get bigger. They can grow to a height of 2m.
5. When the sunflower has finished being a flower, you will be left with a big, round 'plate' of seeds in the middle. When no one's around, tweak out some seeds to give the sunflower a smiley face. You could even give a row of sunflowers different smiles.

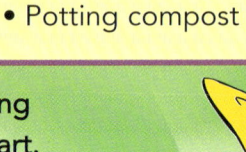

TIP
Give them a tweet! Save your sunflower seeds and feed them to the garden birds.

Micro Makes

Fruit squelch

A fab fresh fruit drink – halfway between squish and squash. Fresh fruit is really good for you. And this recipe is smoooooth! So, why not not have a change from eating fruit the way you normally do and try it like this?

what you need

- A liquidiser
- Some soft fruit
- Small pot of plain yoghurt
- A knife
- A fridge
- A glass

what you do

1. Begin by washing your hands thoroughly.
2. Take up to three types of fruit, such as strawberries, bananas and mango.
3. Peel the fruit (if necessary). Then chop it.
4. Put the fruit and the yoghurt in the liquidiser. Liquidise the whole lot until it turns into a beautifully smooth mush.
5. Tip it into a glass and put it in the fridge.
6. After twenty minutes, take it out of the fridge. Now slurp it down.

Well I never!

When American fruit growers are sorting cranberries to find out which ones are ripe, they sometimes bounce them. It's said that a fully ripe cranberry can be bounced and dribbled just like a basketball!

SERVING SUGGESTIONS

Decorate with fruit and umbrellas (cocktail sort, not full-size) and add a straw. Or add honey to make a sweet, sticky great mess.

Q What's green, juicy, 10,000km long and 12m high?

A The grape wall of China

Micro Makes

Cuddly vampire bat sock puppet

A brilliant way to keep your hand in with your puppetry skills, entertain your pals (and terrify your little sister).

What you need

- An old black sock (preferably not too smelly!)
- A plastic fizzy drink or water bottle
- Glue
- Scraps of black and white paper or felt material
- Scissors
- A black polythene bin liner
- An elastic band
- A red pen or red crayon
- A needle and thread

Smelly socks and cheesy feet ...

You will use a nice 'fragrant' sock for that puppet, won't you? Feet can get sweaty and smelly quite quickly because unwashed feet attract a certain type of foot fungus – it's a close relative of the one that gives Stilton cheese its blue 'veins' and peculiar pong.

Nylon socks and plastic shoes make your feet smell because man-made materials don't allow your feet to 'breathe'. If you want to keep your footsies fresh and fragrant all day, the best things to wear are leather shoes and socks in natural materials, like cotton or wool.

It's a fact!

A single little brown bat can eat 600 mosquitoes in one hour (but without the fries).

What you do

1. Cut off the top quarter of the bottle, including the screw top.

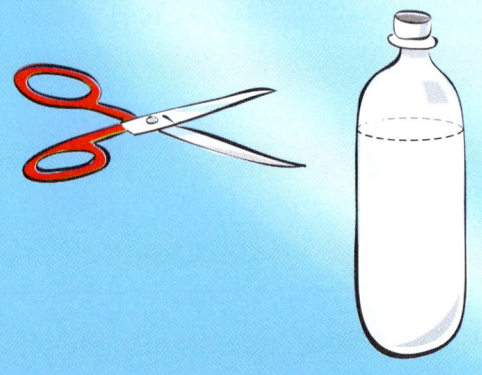

2. Insert the top of the bottle into the toe of the sock. This will be the bat's head.

3. Cut two triangles from the black felt or paper for the bat's ears. Make a little slit in the middle of the long side of each ear. Fold one side of the cut over the other and stick down to make a curved shape.

TIP

To give your bat a really evil look, just cut out the eyes from a magazine or newspaper photo of a well-known politician or dodgy figure from history, e.g. Ghengis Khan, Tony Blair, Rasputin, William Hague.

A spooky story

One moonlit night, two men decided to take a shortcut through a graveyard. They were about halfway through it when they heard a tap-tap-tapping noise coming from the shadows. They peered into the darkness and saw an old man with a hammer and chisel chipping away at one of the gravestones.

When their hearts had finally stopped thumping, one of the men said to him, 'You didn't half give us a scare! We thought you were a ghost or something!'

'Anyway', said his friend 'what are you doing working here this late at night?'.

'Those idiots!' muttered the old man, as he continued chiselling away, 'They spelled my name wrong!'

4. Glue or stitch the ears to the top of the head at the sides. Cut two eye shapes from white paper or card, then draw a red pupil on them for that wicked look. Glue them on.

5. Now make the wings. Cut a wide strip from a bin liner then scrunch it up in the middle and wrap your elastic band around the scrunched bit. Fasten the scrunched bit to the bat's neck with a couple of stitches or a blob of glue.

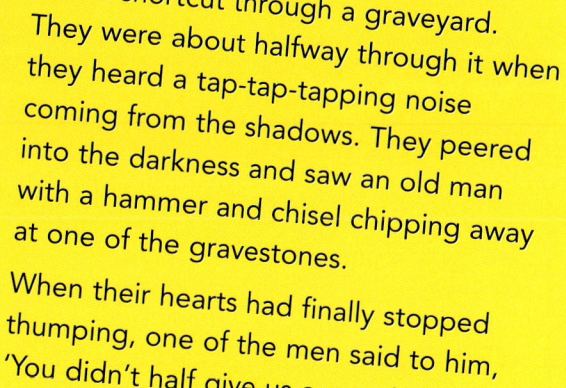

6. Animate your bat. Stick your hand up the sock. Put your fingers in the bottle top then stick your thumb in the bit below and waggle it around so that it looks like the bat's lower jaw.

TIP

You can make different animals by putting different shaped containers into different sizes and colours of socks.

Test it. Leap out at yourself with it! If you scream in terror you've more or less got it right.

Micro Makes

Chocolate chip vanilla cookies

Do yourself a flavour with a Micro-Bake!
Wicked bikkies, 'choc' full of tongue-teasing brown nuggets which just melt in your mouth. When it comes to the crunch ... they can't be licked!

what you need

- 150g of self-raising flour
- 75g of margarine
- 75g of soft brown sugar
- a few drops of vanilla essence
- a little cooking oil
- 100g of milk chocolate chopped up small (or use chocolate chips)
- one egg
- a pinch of salt
- **equipment:**
  an apron
  kitchen scales
  a mixing bowl
  a wooden spoon
  a baking tray

About chips – the bitter truth!

If someone is full of resentment, bitter and jealous we say that they have 'a chip on their shoulder'. Back in the old days in the USA, thug types who were spoiling for a fight in a saloon would pick up a chip of wood from the floor and put it on their shoulder. This was a fighting challenge to anyone who fancied having a go at knocking it off.

what you do

1. Wash your hands really thoroughly. Pre-heat the oven to gas mark 4 (180°C or 350°F).

2. 'Cream' your sugar and margarine together. This means you put them in the bowl and beat them together until the mixture has gone all light and fluffy.

3. Add the egg to the mixture. Break the egg shell by tapping it sharply on the side of the bowl. Then let the contents slither into the mixture. Now beat the eggs in.

4. Beat in the vanilla essence and then gently stir in the flour, salt and chocolate or chocolate chips.

Q What's maroon, tasty, and plays in the Premier Division?

A Aston Vanilla!

Micro Makes

5 Smear a tiny drop of cooking oil all over the baking tray. Put little dollops of cookie mixture on the tray. Make sure they have breathing space as, while they are baking, they will spread. Use oven gloves to put the tray in the oven.

6 After the cookies have been in the oven 10–15 minutes, use an oven glove to remove your baking tray and cookies from the oven. Your cookies will be ready for munching as soon as they're cool.

WARNING!
Take great care not to burn yourself while moving things in or out of a hot oven. Ask a grown-up for help.

Chocolate – some tasty tidbits

Chocolate is made from varying mixtures of cocoa paste, cocoa butter, sugar and milk, depending on whether you're making plain, milk or white chocolate. Cocoa (which has nothing to do with coconuts), is made from the seeds of the cacao or chocolate tree and is bitter tasting. It's the sugar that makes it sweet.

Cocoa for drinking was first brought to Britain from South America in the 17th Century. South American Indians have been chocoholics for hundreds of years; the Aztecs called their cocoa drink 'chocolatl'. People in Britain didn't get the idea of making solid chocolate for eating until the 1900s.

COMEDY CORNER

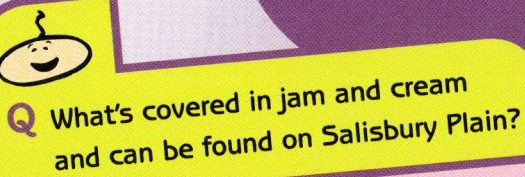

Q What's tall, sweet and wobbly and stands in the middle of Paris?
A The Trifle Tower

Q What's covered in jam and cream and can be found on Salisbury Plain?
A Sconehenge

Micro Makes

Feisty face lifts

This is a great way to improve your drawing skills and powers of observation – all done with lots and lots of half measures.

what you need

- A biggish portrait photograph from a magazine – could be your favourite pop star, film or TV celebrity, sports hero .... or politician? The best sorts of portraits to use are the ones that are more or less symmetrical, that means where the person is looking straight ahead. (The worst sort are the ones where they've got their head in a paper bag!).
- A ruler
- A pencil
- A pair of scissors
- Some sketching pencils or artist's oil pastels (but ask the artist first!)
- A piece of white paper or thin card a bit bigger than the photograph you've chosen

What you do

1. Cut the picture out of the magazine or colour supplement (but not your library book!).

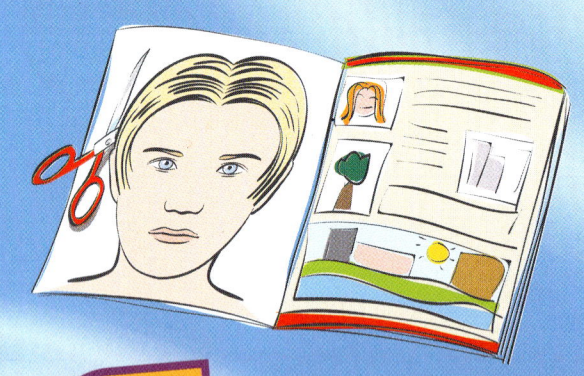

He's a terrible artist! He can't even draw his curtains!

2. Use your ruler to draw a vertical line exactly down the centre of the photograph so that it more or less bisects ('divides in two') the whole face.

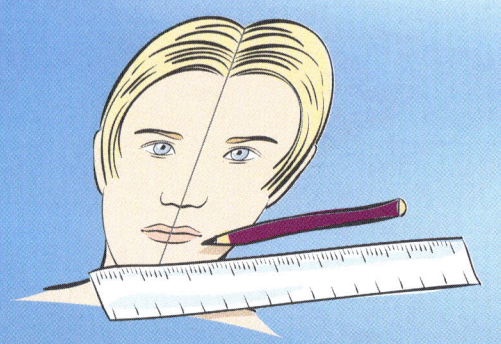

Q How do you carve a statue of a horse?

A Easy! Just get a block of stone and chip off all the bits that DON'T look like a horse.

Xchange

Micro Makes

3) Cut the picture straight down the line so that you split the face in two (now apologise to your hero for so cruelly mutilating his/her lovely face!)

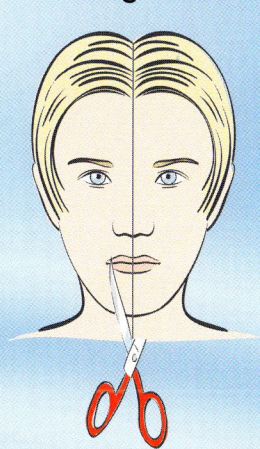

Another idea

Why not do a self portrait? For this you will obviously need a photograph of yourself. Don't bother looking for this in magazines (unless you happen to be quite famous).

TIP
Draw a frame around your finished portrait if you like.

4) Glue half of the face to one side of your piece of paper or card.

5) Now use your pencils or pastels to draw very carefully the missing side of the face. As you work, keep looking back at the photograph.

Pencil facts both totally pointless!

If you use a normal pencil carefully it's possible to write about 50,000 English words with it! Alternatively, if you just drew a continuous line with your pencil, it would be thirty five miles long (the line, not the pencil) before the pencil was used up.

- Check overall face shape.
- Check skin and hair colour (OK ... so they're bald!)
- Check expression ... happy? sad? dim? slimy?
- Check shape of lips, nose, eyes, ears.
- Check those subtle shadows that give shape and substance to features.
- Check for interesting extra facial features e.g. moustaches, beards, scars, freckles, warts.
- Check accessories – specs, earrings, nose rings.

Micro Makes

Xchange

Create a fabulous widescreen photorama

Have you ever seen a breathtakingly beautiful landscape and wanted to take a gigantic great photo of it, only to look through your camera's viewfinder and find the image looks like nothing more than a postage stamp-sized picture even a short-sighted ant wouldn't look at twice?

Here's a fabulous, fun way to create a huge, spectacular and brilliantly detailed 'photorama' of your favourite subject. And it's not just the perfect way to capture for all time fabulous seascapes, cityscapes and landscapes. You can also use it to create an amazing 'photorama' of any other large subject, such as your street, garden, school playground, local sports ground or anything else you like!

what you do

1. Choose your subject.
2. Stand on a spot in front of it. The really important thing is to keep your feet in exactly the same position for the whole time you're taking photos.
3. Look through the camera's viewfinder and 'pan' – this means slowly swinging the camera from one side to the other, as well as up and down. When you have finished panning you'll have a good idea of all the things you will include in your mega-pic.
4. You're going to divide up your photorama into equal rectangular segments. Each photograph you take will be one of these segments and will go to build up your final mega-pic.
5. Get ready to shoot. Remember to keep your camera as steady as you can. If your camera wobbles when you click you'll get blurry pictures.

what you need

- A camera with a film in it
- Glue
- A big sheet of card

TIP
Some photographers actually hold their breath when they snap so you could try doing that (but not for too long!).

Micro Makes

6 Start by taking the first photo at the far left area of your panorama. Swing your camera slightly to the right for the next 'segment' of the picture. It doesn't matter if you include a sliver of the previous shot. Click again, then swing on one more segment. Carry on until you have covered the whole scene.

- To make your picture taller, move your camera up a frame, then repeat the left to right snapping process. You could include a really dramatic sky.
- Alternatively, drop your camera down a frame and photograph the lower area.

8 Get your photos developed.

9 Now for the really exciting bit! Lay the photos out on a flat surface and match them up until you've got the big picture! It's like a assembling a photographic jigsaw that has rectangular pieces.

TIP A cheapo disposable camera will do just as well for this project.

10 Glue the 'photorama' down onto the big piece of card.

Gasp at a your own brilliance!

Exhibit your work on your bedroom wall.

Rush off to find your next subject!

Micro Makes

Xchange

Make your own marvellous miniature garden paradise

This is a sort of 'Ground Force' meets 'Honey I Shrunk the Lawnmower' meets 'Changing Gnomes' project. It's lots of fun to do, especially if you like designing and making things. And when you've finished you can hire a miniature gardener to help keep the whole thing tidy for you!

Stage one – planning

what you need

- A sheet of paper. If you want to be really professional, you could use the squared stuff the experts use.
- A pencil, a rubber, some coloured pencils
- A decent ruler (Henry II? Queen Elizabeth I?)
- Some imagination (available in all good heads)

What you do

1. Decide what you want in your mini-garden. Here are some suggestions: a greenhouse; a shed; paths; a gravelled drive; a pond; a swimming pool; a lawn; some wooden 'decking'; flower beds (flowers get tired too, you know); a woodland or wildlife area.

2. Draw a plan of your garden. Think carefully about the best places for all the stuff you'll put in it – you wouldn't want a pond right outside the back door!

Stage two – the creation

what you need

- Bottle tops
- Foil
- Soil
- Plasticine or blue tack
- Strips of card
- Twigs
- Glue
- A large, shallow tray
- Used matchsticks or tooth picks
- Small dried flowers or petals
- Gravel, stones and pebbles
- Small pictures of clothes from magazines
- Clear plastic drinks bottle
- Small plastic container lid e.g. small margarine tub lid
- Moss (but only from your own garden or a garden centre. It's illegal to take it from the wild)
- Small seeds (optional)

Micro Makes

What you do

1. Divide your tray into the areas you drew on your plan. You can do this by taping strips of card to the base of the tray. However if you're really careful, this isn't absolutely necessary.
2. Set out 'lawns' of moss (or sow grass seed on soil).
3. Make flower beds with soil. They'll work best if it's really fine soil, that is, not lumpy. If you want real things growing in your mini-garden, try adding very small seeds, like mustard and cress, to your soil. If you do this, remember to keep the soil moist.

Here are just a few ideas to get you started

Once your imagination gets going you'll probably come up with lots of your own ideas. You may get so brilliant at this sort of thing that you end up as one of the top garden designers of the future.

Glue small dried flowers or petals to matchsticks or tooth picks for your flowers.

Cut the bottom from a transparent drinks bottle to make a domed greenhouse.

Lay paths using stones and pebbles.

Plant trees by pushing twigs into plasticine.

Make miniature tubs and plant pots out of bottle tops.

Cover a plastic container lid in foil to make a garden pond.

Make a rock garden using small stones and pebbles.

Make a washing line with two twigs and a bit of string. Cut out clothes to go on it from magazines then stick them on the string.

Well I never!

There are a million ants for every human being in the world. So, would you like yours now, or later?

Warning!

Now that you have got your miniature garden, prepare to be invaded by miniature TV gardeners, desperate to give your creation the make-over once-over.

Micro Makes

Scrummy spud and bacon cakes

Here's a great way to make yourself a tasty brekky, brunch, lunch or tea with a difference, using leftover spuds and what-not. Incidentally, if the shops round your way don't have 'what-not', use the ingredients listed below (they'll taste better anyway).

what you need

- About 250g leftover cooked potatoes
- 50g butter
- a drop of cooking oil
- 100g self raising flour plus a bit more for rolling in (the spuds, not you)
- Salt and pepper
- 55ml of milk or cream
- A couple of rashers of cooked bacon
- Baking tray, mixing bowl, fork, knife

Tatty facts

Potatoes produce their own electricity. Just two potatoes would knock out enough electricity to run a 'potato clock', but to power an electric light bulb you'd need about 480 spuds.

Serving suggestion

Have your tatty cakes with scrambled or fried eggs, sausage, beans, bacon and mushrooms...

Mmmm

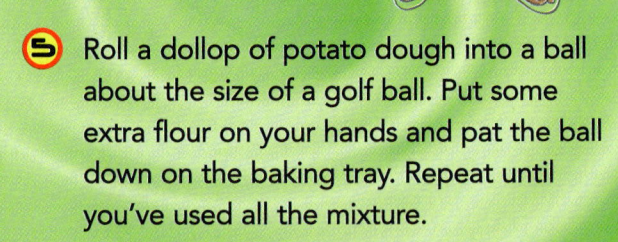

What you do

1. Wash your hands and pre-heat the oven to gas mark 5 (190°C or 375°F).

2. Mash up the potatoes and butter in the mixing bowl using a fork. Chop the cooked bacon and add it to the potato mixture with the salt and pepper.

3. Bung in 100g of the flour and the milk (or cream), then mix the whole lot up until you get a nice soft dough.

4. Smear a tiny drop of cooking oil all over the baking tray to stop the spud and bacon cakes sticking.

5. Roll a dollop of potato dough into a ball about the size of a golf ball. Put some extra flour on your hands and pat the ball down on the baking tray. Repeat until you've used all the mixture.

6. Using the oven gloves put the baking tray in the oven. After about ten minutes, take the spud and bacon cakes out.

Micro Makes

Say it with flowers

What a great way to surprise and delight your family, friends, neighbours, local bees, passing helicopter pilots, vultures, etc with a spring message. You do this one in the autumn – in other words, the time of year when the leaves lose their trees.

what you need

- Some crocus bulbs (a small spring flower)
- A lawn or flower bed
- Some pebbles
- A garden trowel
- A day when everyone's out (not you though)

TIP
Fun variations on this planting theme include: 'cartooning', or 'painting' with your bulbs to make fabulous flowery masterpieces

What you do

1. Decide on your message. Keep the message short for best effect – just someone's name or initials is good.

2. Write your message on the grass or soil with the pebbles to see how looks. You need to make your writing a minimum of 25cm high. Obviously, the bigger your writing, the more bulbs you will need.

3. Try to look at your writing from a height to get an overview. Use an upstairs window, if you have one.

4. Now plant your crocus bulbs where the pebbles are. Using the trowel, dig little holes about 3cm apart. The holes should be about twice the depth of the bulbs. Place the bulbs in the holes, make sure you get the growing tip at the top. Cover with soil.

5. Tidy away the pebbles. Also, if you removed bits of turf from the lawn, put them back now so there is absolutely no trace of what you've been doing.

6. Wait for spring to come. To pass the time while you're waiting, do things like going to school, having Hallowe'en, Christmas etc.

Important!
Do not be tempted to dig up your bulbs in order to find out how they're doing; they won't like this one bit!

Micro Makes

Beanie baby

A little bundle of joy to hug, cuddle and call your own. Forever full of beans .... but always as good as gold.

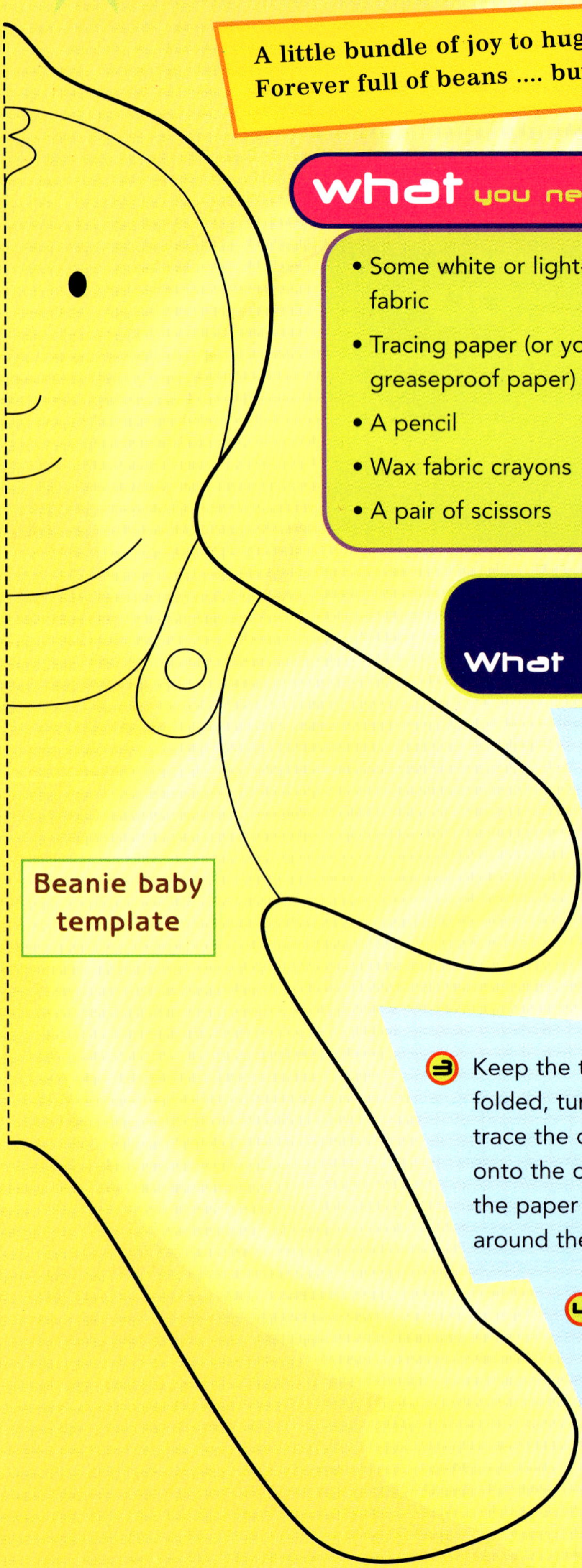

what you need

- Some white or light-coloured fabric
- Tracing paper (or you can use greaseproof paper)
- A pencil
- Wax fabric crayons
- A pair of scissors
- A needle and some thread
- An iron – it's best to use the sort that comes with a ready-fitted adult, as it's safer
- Some dried beans, rice, lentils or polystyrene beads to stuff your baby with.

Beanie baby template

what you do

1. Fold your tracing paper.

2. Place the fold on the dotted line on the left edge of the beanie baby template. Trace the outline, face and clothes onto your tracing paper.

3. Keep the tracing paper folded, turn it over and trace the details through onto the other side. With the paper still folded, cut around the outline.

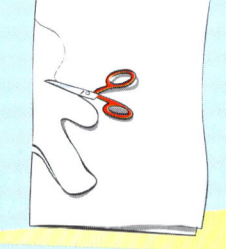

4. Repeat stages 1–3, only don't trace the face. Draw the back of the clothes (see next step). Now you have a tracing **paper front and back for your baby.**

16 Xchange — Micro Makes

5. Use your fabric crayons to colour the details of your baby's face, body and clothes onto the paper. You can copy this picture for the back of the baby. Try to get a thick coat of crayon on the paper.

6. Place the coloured shapes crayon side down on the fabric. Then, with the help of an adult, iron over them following the instructions on your crayons.

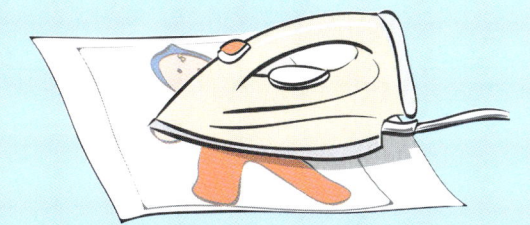

7. When you lift up your paper, the ironing should have transferred the crayon beanie baby images to the fabric. Leaving a border of about 1 ½ cm all the way round the edges, cut them out.

8. Put the two sides of the baby together with the coloured sides facing inwards! Now begin to sew them together along the outline of the coloured shape that you can see through the fabric. Use small stitches so that your baby won't 'spill beans'. Leave about 6cm unsewn.

9. At the moment your baby is 'inside out'. Carefully turn it so that the coloured sides are facing outwards.

10. Now, using the left-open gap, stuff your baby with beans or whatever else you've decided to use. Do it so that it's nicely padded and scrunchy.

11. Now sew up the gap with small, close together stitches.

Well I never!

You're born with about three hundred bones but by the time you've become a grown up you've only got about two hundred. Don't worry! You don't actually lose them or anything dramatic like that. What happens is that quite a few bones in a baby's body are in sections but, as the baby grows, they join together to form just one bone.

Important note!

Whatever you do, don't overdo the stuffing. The last thing you want is your baby exploding!

Please don't try to wash your baby. If you filled it with rice or beans, water will make them swell!

Micro Makes

Xchange 17

Sexton Blake ... fake!

Here's how to whip up an amazing old master art forgery. Sexton Blake was the name of a popular storybook detective, and it's also the Cockney rhyming slang for a fake. If you think you're up to producing a Sexton Blake, take a few tips on how to do it ... but only if you're crafty enough!

Important
Even if you consider yourself bad at drawing, the following method for copying a picture works a treat.

what you need

- Some drawing paper. The best to use is 'cartridge' paper, the posh sort that artists use.
- A postcard or some other copy of an 'old master' drawing (not a coloured painting) – maybe one that you've cut from a magazine.
- A soft pencil – about B or 2B
- A ruler
- A soft paintbrush
- Some instant coffee
- A pen to make your drawing with
- A hair dryer, or radiator.
- Some sandpaper
- A damp cloth.

Part one – forge ahead

What you do

1. Take your 'original' and draw a grid pattern on it using your ruler and pencil. Draw a line down the middle then another one across the middle. Divide the four resulting rectangles into two, and so on and so forth until your picture is broken into lots of equal sized 'squares'.

2. Draw a grid on your big piece of paper in the same way you did on your 'original' picture. Each square on the original will correspond to a bigger square on your copy, which makes copying really easy.

   Important – your paper should be **exactly** two, three or four times bigger than the original so that the proportions correspond.

TIP
Use your soft pencil to do this grid because later on you are going to rub it out.

Micro Makes

3. Now, using your pen, get drawing. Copy a square at a time. The overall composition of the picture will take care of itself and should be a doddle ... or a doodle!

4. Carefully rub the grid pattern off the forgery.

Part two – ageing

What you do

TIP
It doesn't necessarily have to be a head – it could be a still life, landscape, animal picture ... whatever you like really.

1. It's time to start ageing the picture. Mix up half a teaspoon of the instant coffee in some warm water.

2. Using your big, soft brush, gently brush over the entire surface of your picture with the coffee. Dry it off using the hair dryer or leave it on a radiator to dry.

3. Give your picture some 'fox' marks – the 'fox coloured' reddish-brown marks that appear on old pictures. Dab your damp cloth on the picture. Take a tiny pinch of coffee granules and carefully throw them up in the air so they fall at random on the the picture. They will dissolve and make dark splodges. Now dry the paper again.

4. Age your masterpiece more by laying a piece of sandpaper on the table and rubbing the paper's edges on it until they look worn. Then nick the corners with your thumbnail.

5. Sign the picture – preferably with the original artist's name, not your own, as that might just give the game away (or why not just sign it: Fay Kingham?)

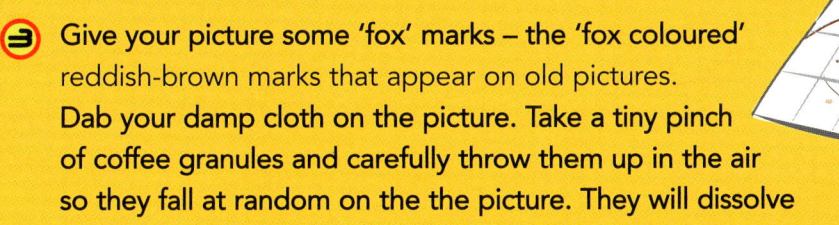

WELL I NEVER

The Victorian artist and creator of nonsense rhymes, Edward Lear, saved himself a fortune in blotting paper by teaching his pet cat to roll across the wet ink on his paper.

Doh!

The Dutch forger, Hans van Meegeren, painted two fakes of 'masterpieces' by the Dutch artist, Vermeer, and sold them to a nasty Nazi called Hermann Göering. Hans thought he'd done pretty well out of the deal until he discovered that Hermann had paid him for the pictures with fake money!

Micro Makes

A gorgeous garden lantern

To light up your lilies, dazzle your daffodils and put a shine on your shrubs!
A 'can'-do project!

what you need

- A food can e.g. tinned tomatoes, beans or carrots
- Some water – available at all good outlets (or 'taps', as most people call them)
- A felt-tip marker with 'permanent' ink – that's the sort that doesn't wash off
- A freezer
- A soft surface – something like an old towel or sweater
- Different-sized nails (the knocking in wood type from DIY stores) and a hammer
- A night light – a short, fat candle – you can buy these at hardware shops
- Matches

WARNING! Make sure the can has no jagged edges that you might cut your fingers on.

'Can' we have the facts?

Tin cans were invented in the early 1800s, but the first proper can opener wasn't invented until 1885. Soldiers in the Crimean War opened their cans of nosh with their bayonets and, if that didn't work, they just shot them with their rifles!

what you do

1. Wash the can. Remove the label. If the glue from the label is difficult to shift, scrub it off with warm water, soap and a scourer.

2. Using your felt-tip pen, draw a pattern of dots on the can – you decide on the pattern. Get creative! Fill the can with water, then put it in your freezer. Leave until the next day, when it should be frozen solid.

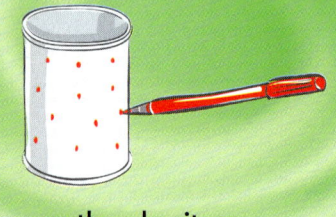

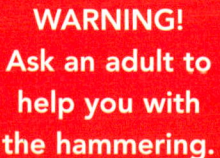

WARNING! Ask an adult to help you with the hammering.

3. Take the can out of the freezer, then lay it on the old towel or sweater. Use the hammer and nails to punch holes in the can where you marked the spots with the felt-tip.

4. Put the can in a bowl or sink and let the ice melt. Empty the water away. Leave the can to dry.

BE CAREFUL! The inside of the can will now have sharp edges.

Important!

Ask an adult to put the night light carefully in the can for you, and light it.

OK! Glow, can, glow! The flickering effect will make interesting patterns and drive local moths crazy.

Micro Makes

Images with impact

Make a fantastic photomontage of magic moments. Lying around somewhere, you've probably got a whole load of photos that mean a lot to you. For instance, they might be pictures recording all those magic moments in the life of your pet cat, such as her first fur ball, birthday party, visit to the vet, (sparrow sandwich?) – that sort of thing. Why not have them on permanent display by creating a 'photomontage'?

what you need

- A medium-sized clip frame.
- Lots of snaps of your chosen subject. This can be anything really – perhaps something to do with your hobbies and interests, such as photos or postcards of dolls, cars, footballers etc.
- Scissors
- Blue tack
- An adult (to help you with the clip frame).

What you do

1. Read the instructions on the clip frame, then ask an adult to remove the clips and glass.

2. Lay the backing board on a flat surface and arrange your pics on it. Get creative and jiggle them around a bit to achieve the most effective arrangement. Maybe overlap the edges, or even trim the background from some of the pictures, in order to emphasise the bits you want to focus on.

3. Once you've arranged the photographs exactly as you want them, use little blobs of blue tack to hold them firmly in place. Now, with the help of an adult again, replace the glass and clips.

Important warning!
Sheets of glass are really, really dangerous! They must be handled with care. Use an adult to dismantle and reassemble the clip frame.

Bright Idea!

You could even include bits of 'memorabilia' in your montage. For instance, if you were doing a sort of 'This is your life' in pictures montage for your pet cat, dog, (yak?) you could bung in some 'non-photographic' stuff like their old collar, name disc, or vaccination certificate.

TIP
Leave some of the photos complete - especially the ones around the edges of the arrangement.

Micro Makes

Something 'buzzy'

Next time you think you know the answer in a quiz game, do it like they do on TV and radio. Hot wire yourself and the other contestants with a few of these fantastic little gizmos! They're cheap, easy to make and will give your quiz a real buzz!

what you need

- A battery 4.5 volts ... or bigger
- At least two little buzzers, between 3 and 6 volts each. Try to get ones that make different sounds.
- Wire cutters and strippers
- Scissors
- Thin card cut into small pieces
- Electrical wire – single core sort
- Paper fasteners
- Some ingenuity (brains!)

what you do

1. **First test your buzzer.** Use the wire strippers to strip about 2cm of the plastic covering from the ends of the wires which are attached to the buzzer. Now attach the wires to the battery terminals. If the buzzer buzzes, you're wired for action but if it doesn't, swap the wires around.

2. **Extend the buzzer wires.** Un-hitch the buzzer wires from the battery. Cut two lengths of wire and strip each end of both. Join your new lengths to the buzzer wires by 'twisting' their ends together.

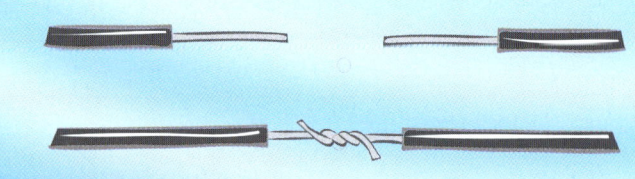

Mrs. Watt: Wire you insulate?

Mr. Watt (an electrician): I couldn't get Ohm earlier.

TIP
You can probably get almost all of these bits and pieces from a hardware shop, DIY superstore or electrical supplies shop.

Micro Makes

3. **Make a switch.** Cut out a piece of card (about 8cm by 3cm) then fold it in two. Next, make a hole through both halves of the card. Push a paper fastener through each hole so that the pointy ends are on the outside of the folded card. When you press the card down, the round tops of the paper fasteners should touch.

5. **Join the switch into the circuit.** Join one of the wires from the switch to the wire from the buzzer, and the other to the battery. When you press the card down, the circuit will be complete. This allows the electricity to flow all the way round the circuit and makes the buzzer buzz.

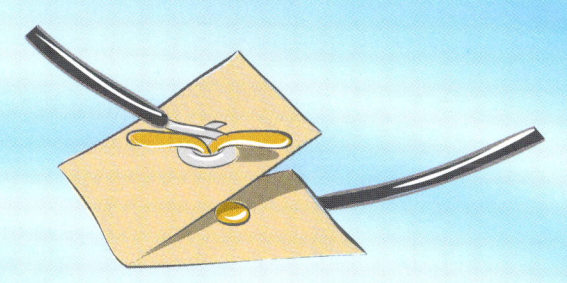

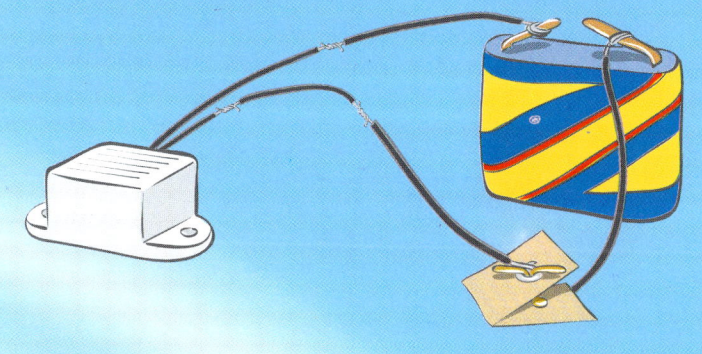

4. Cut two more pieces of wire and strip both ends of each one. Attach one piece of wire to each paper fastener by twisting it around the flattened pointy ends on the outside of the card.

6. **Make another buzzer.** You can do this by repeating the process and attaching the buzzer wires to the same battery, or you could get another battery.

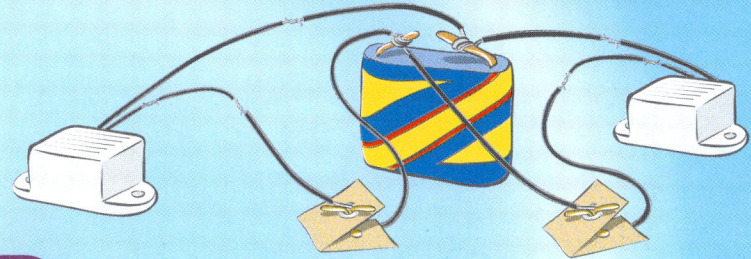

Negative and positive thinking

While he was trying to invent a battery to store electricity, the inventor, Thomas Alva Edison (1847–1931) did 50 000 unsuccessful experiments before hitting on the answer.

When someone said that 50 000 failed experiments was a high price to pay to achieve results, Thomas replied, 'Results? Why I have gotten a lot of results. I now know 50 000 things that won't work.'

You're in buzzness!

Now all you need is a couple of ~~victims~~ contestants and you can have a quiz. You can choose almost any subject: general knowledge, sport, pop music – only make sure you know the correct answers! You can find quizzes in books, too. Try looking in the *Xchange Headstrong* book for some good ones.

Micro Makes

Shear magic – a topiary bird

Topiary is a cross between sculpture, hairdressing and horticulture (posh word for gardening), where all sorts of interesting animals and objects are created from shrubs and bushes. It's great fun and you can do it! Here's how to grow, train and make your very own topiary bird.

Warning! That wire's dangerous stuff. Keep it away from your own eyes and those of other people!

What you need

- Some wire – strong but bendable.
- A pair of wire cutters
- Some garden twist ties – little plastic coated bits of wire
- Some gravel
- An ivy plant (inexpensive)
- A plant pot (even cheaper)
- Scissors (an absolute snip!)
- Potting compost or soil (dirt cheap!)
- A pair of pliers

What you do

1. Carefully bend some of the wire into a bird shape. Use just as much wire as it takes.

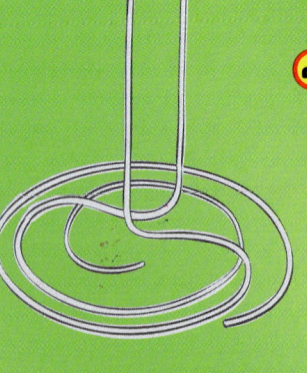

2. Using two other lengths of wire, make a stem and twist a round base for your bird.

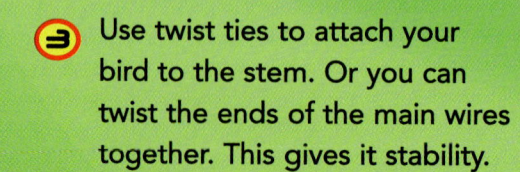

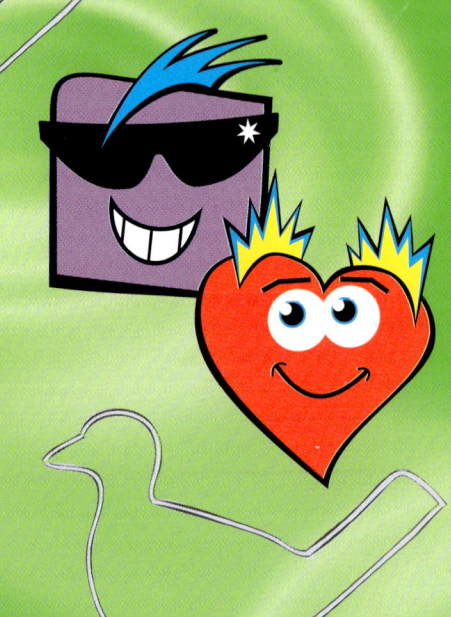

3. Use twist ties to attach your bird to the stem. Or you can twist the ends of the main wires together. This gives it stability.

Micro Makes

4. Place the whole caboodle in the plant pot and put some gravel over the base to make it really secure and steady.

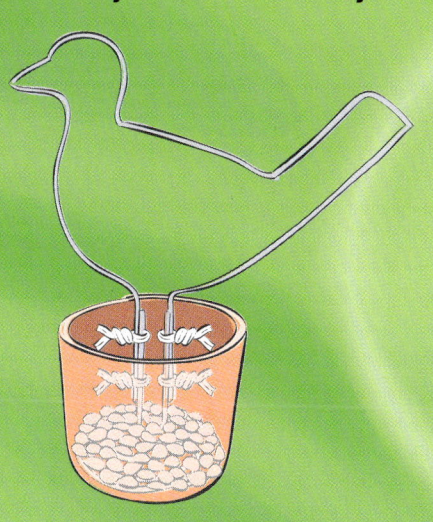

5. Then put soil or compost in the pot and plant your ivy plant in it. Give it a drink of water so that it feels happy and at home. When your ivy plant begins to grow, train it up the central stem of the wire sculpture shape, then on to the bird shape.

6. As your plant continues to grow, keep trimming it. A gentle snip here and there is best. Remember! This is topiary – not the 'All Australia Sheep-Shearing Finals'. So don't overdo it. Just leaf well alone! Where you make a cut, new shoots will grow, quickly covering your frame.

TIP
Occasionally feel the soil in the plant pot to make sure it hasn't dried out. In order to make sure that all the sides of the plant get equal amounts of sunlight, turn it regularly (not _too_ much or it'll get dizzy and fall over).

TIP
This project takes a bit of time, so be patient. Your bird will take a few months to grow. We're talking ivy – not Jack's Beanstalk!

Suggestions for ambushious topiarists: Instead of making a bird you could make a topiary dog, orangutan, fish, amoeba, vampire, camel ... maybe even a bush?

More ideas
If you like, you could have a bash at some real outdoor topiary and get snipping away at a hedge or shrub in your garden. But don't go turning your mum's prize japonicus spaconicus into a Tyrannosaurus Rex without asking first!

Micro Makes

A fiercesome flapping vampire

Scare yourself and your friends shirtless with this vile vampire! It's slightly more tricky than some of the other 'makes' so you'll need to follow the stages carefully.

I come from Transylvania

Of your **blood** I'm gonna drain ya

Oh what the heck ... here's me neck

I'm a sucker for Vampiremania!

what you need

- A sheet of white card – A4 size
- A pencil
- A ruler
- A pair of scissors
- A hole punch (or half a slap?)
- 2 split-pin type paper fasteners
- Some sticky tape
- Some wool, thin string or thick cotton
- A piece of black polythene – you can cut this from a bin liner
- Felt-tip pens, crayons or paints

What you do

1 Fold the A4 card lengthwise.

2 Draw a line about 3cm from the side of your card. Cut along the line through both layers of card. The two strips of card will be your vampire's arms.

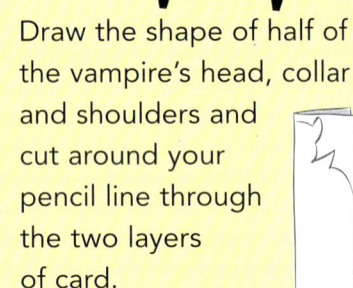

3 Draw the shape of half of the vampire's head, collar and shoulders and cut around your pencil line through the two layers of card.

4 Unfold the vampire shape.

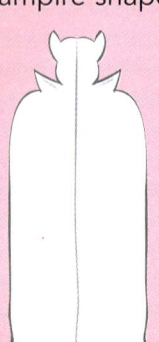

5 Draw hands on the ends of the arm strips. Cut round the fingers.

6 Punch a hole in each arm, about 3cm down from the top.

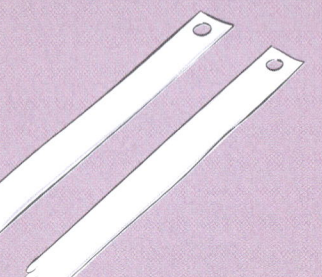

Xchange — Micro Makes

7 Lay the arms on the back of the vampire. Put a pencil point through the holes to mark where they are. Push the pencil point through the marks to make holes. Push the split pins through the body, then the arms, from the front.

8 Spread the pins' 'arms' out. Tape some string from the top of one arm to the top of the other so that it is taut when the arms are down.

9 Tie about 35cm of string to the centre of the first length of string.

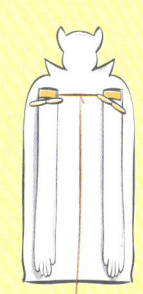

10 Test that the vampire flaps by pulling gently on the hanging string. The arms should lift up.

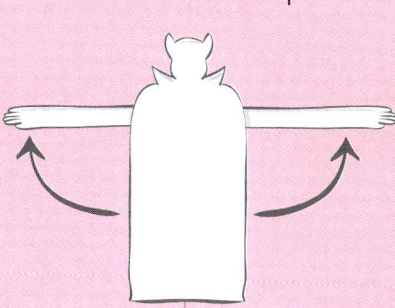

11 Neckst! Cut two identical triangles of 'wing skin' (or 'cloak' if you're a softy) from black polythene. Make them right-angled triangles by cutting the corners off a square shape.

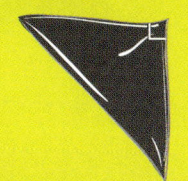

12 Stick one edge of 'wing skin' to the back of the each arm. Make sure the right angles are nearest the body end of the arms.

13 Now get arty and draw, paint or collage a face and some clothes for your vampire! You may wish to model your vampire on someone you know? Your head teacher? That woman in the sweet shop (yes, the one who's got no shadow)?

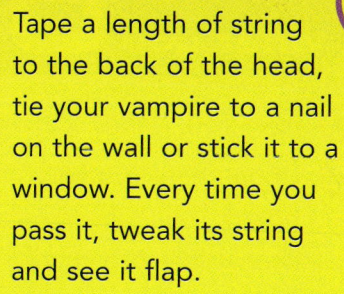

14 Tape a length of string to the back of the head, tie your vampire to a nail on the wall or stick it to a window. Every time you pass it, tweak its string and see it flap.

Micro Makes

Xchange 27

Groovy garlic bread

Garlic bread that's guaranteed to gobsmack ghouls and titillate taste buds!

Fact! Garlic is good for you! The Ancient Egyptians worshipped it and Olympian athletes chewed it. This amazingly helpful herb protects you from all sorts of things, including colds and coughs, bacteria, heart disease ... and rampaging vampires.

what you need

- A French stick loaf – these are sometimes called baguettes. But you don't have to go all the way to France for one. You can get them in most supermarkets and bakeries.
- Some cloves of garlic – the pods that pong
- About 50g of butter
- Some parsley or other herbs (optional)
- Some baking foil
- A sharp knife – be really careful with this!
- A chopping board
- A garlic crusher (not essential)

TIP
If it's straight out of the fridge, your butter will be hard so you'll need to soften it by leaving it somewhere warm for a while, such as near a radiator, on a window sill (or in Saudi Arabia?)

What you do

1. Give your hands a thorough wash.
2. Chop chop! Put your bread on the bread board, then take the sharp knife and chop it vertically into chunks about 3cm long.
3. Peel your garlic cloves then crush or chop them. Mix your crushed or chopped garlic with the butter, then add your parsley or herbs, if you're using them. Spread the butter lightly on the cut surfaces of the bread.
4. Reassemble your bread chunks into a stick loaf on top of the foil. Wrap the foil around it and bung it in a hot oven for about ten minutes.
5. Eat the garlic bread.

Snog your vampire!

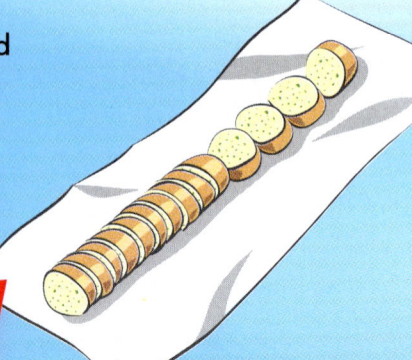

Micro Makes

Send garden birds nuts!

With every year that passes there are fewer and fewer birds around. There are three main reasons for this. **Firstly,** stacks of birds get clobbered by pet cats. **Secondly,** lots of bird environments are being destroyed to make room for yet more roads, houses and factories. **Thirdly,** believe it or not, gardeners still use things like nasty poisonous slug pellets that also poison birds that eat the slugs.

No wonder we hardly see thrushes any more! You can do something to help the birds and encourage them to come into your garden by simply feeding them. Here you can see one really fun way to do this.

Then you can enjoy watching birds like blue tits do all sorts of high-wire acrobatics trying to peck the nuts from the shells.

what you need

- Some 'monkey' nuts (peanuts) still in their shells
- A thick, strong sewing needle. **Be very careful when using a needle!**
- Some strong sewing thread or some slim, strong string (try saying that with a mouthful of monkey nuts!)

Important!
Don't hang the nuts where they can be reached by cats. Sometimes the birds get so excited when they're pecking the nuts that they fail to notice the pesky pussies sneaking up on them.

what you do

1. Thread your needle and tie a large knot in the end of the string or strong thread.
2. Push the needle through the shells in the 'shortest' direction until you have got about 30cm of string threaded with shells.
3. Make a loop at the top of the thread, then hang from a tree, washing line or hook in your garden (the nuts, not you!).
4. Reminder! After the nuts have all been eaten, don't forget to replace them otherwise the birds will think you've just been 'stringing' them along.

Micro Makes

Brilliant beaded bracelet

This great piece of personalised jewellery will cost you hardly anything at all.

Well I never!

The safety pin was invented in 1849 in New York by a man called Walter Hunt. He thought up the idea after he'd been fiddling with a bit of wire. You'd think he'd have had better things to do with his time, wouldn't you?

what you need

What you need
- A large quantity of safety pins.
- Some small beads. You choose the colours and shapes.
- Shearing elastic. It's the sort you can thread and is ideal for this. If you can't get it, the other sort will do … at a stretch.
- Some nimble fingers (preferably your own)

TIP!
If you can't afford to buy beads you can always get them from old necklaces – make sure you ask the owner first, though!

What you do

1. Open a safety pin. Put some beads onto the safety pin. Now close it.

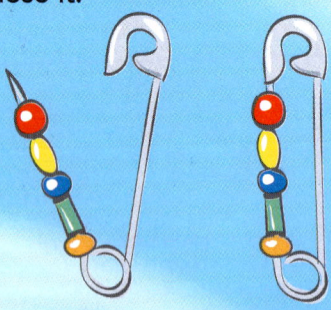

WARNING!
An open pin is no longer a safety pin. It's a danger pin! So keep them away from eyes, balloons, babies' bottoms etc.

2. Repeat this for all the other safety pins. Lay the safety pins in a row, alternate ways up.

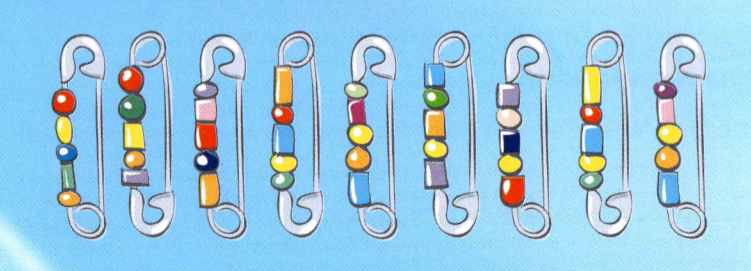

30 Xchange   Micro Makes

④ Now thread the elastic through all the holes in the tops and bottoms of one side of the row of safety pins. While you're doing this, make sure the safety pins hang vertically with the bead side facing you.

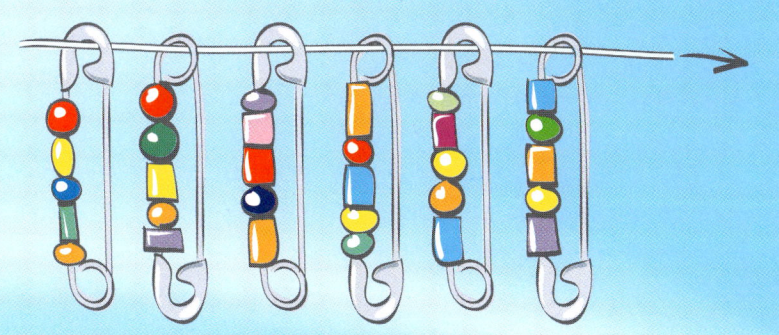

⑤ Repeat the operation, threading the other end of your elastic through the other side of your row of pins.

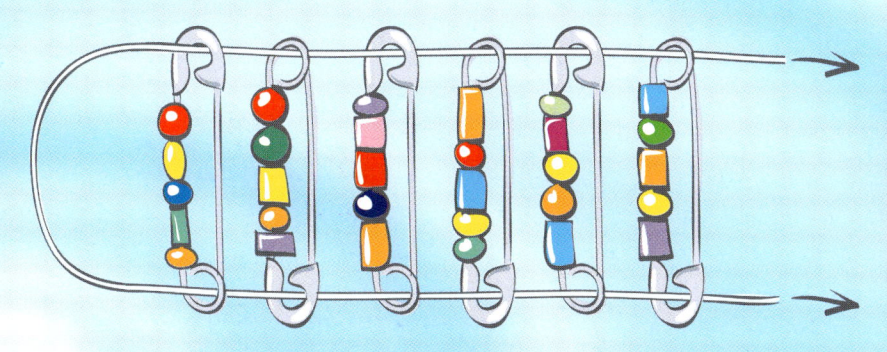

⑥ Holding the elastic carefully, try the bracelet on for size. You could ask a friend to help you hold it.

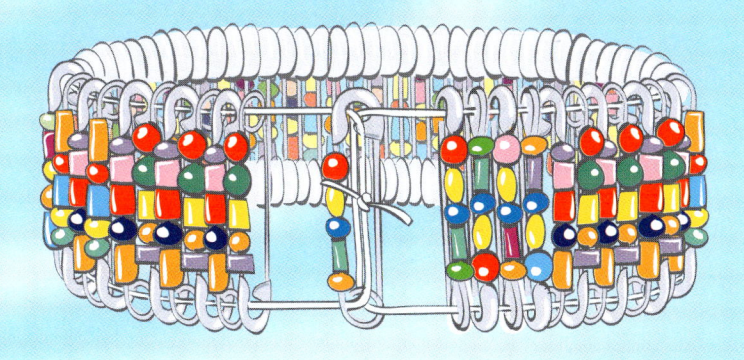

⑦ Thread each end of the elastic through the first safety pin again so that you have a bracelet, rather than a long strip of safety pins.

⑧ When you're happy with your bracelet, tie the ends firmly together. Trim the ends then hide the knot so it doesn't show.

EXTRA IDEAS (FOR OVER-ACHIEVERS)

- Mix and match your bead shapes and colours. Try random or co-ordinated patterns (or go for that much sought-after 'dog's dinner' look).
- Try adding non-beady objects to your bracelet e.g. bits and bobs you've found, such as little washers and nuts (shrunken human skulls? the back axle off a Ford Escort?)
- Use different types and sizes of safety pins, or maybe even gold or silver ones (as used by the Queen when her knicker elastic snaps at Royal receptions).

FLAUNTING TIPS

Look at your watch a lot, wave to complete strangers in the street, run your fingers through your hair, talk into your mobile phone when there's no one there (yes, just as usual).

And finally ... put on your new bracelet and flaunt it!

Micro Makes

Minute mouth-watering mini pizzas

All topping fun! Feel so hungry you could eat a horse then chase the jockey? Here's a great way to satisfy your tum and your need to get creative in the kitchen. Don't sit in front of the goggle box watching telly chefs. Get active! Cook up these scrumptious Italian mini-pizzas.

Q What's tall, golden brown, tilted and covered in mozzarella cheese

A The Leaning Tower of Pizzas

What you need

- Two tablespoons of fresh chopped herbs or a pinch of dried herbs
- Four tablespoons of olive oil
- A packet of puff pastry ready rolled
- One beaten egg
- A CD playing Italian opera music (optional)
- Two tablespoons of tomato purée
- An oven
- Toppings – you decide
- Grated cheese
- A baking tray
- A pastry cutter
- A pastry brush

TIP! Put the CD on really loud. This is to get you in the mood for pizza. You may feel like singing along as you cook.

What you do

1. Wash your hands thoroughly. Pre-heat the oven to 220°C (425°F, gas mark 7).

2. Open out your puff pastry and cut as many rounds, squares or triangles as you can with your pastry cutter. Smear a drop of oil over the baking tray. Brush beaten egg over each pizza base, then place them on the tray.

3. Put them in the oven and cook for about eight minutes until they're golden brown. Take them out of the oven and let them cool slightly.

4. Spread the tomato purée on them as though you were buttering bread. Now you add your favourite toppings e.g. mushrooms, prawns, salami, tuna, olives etc.

5. Mix the chopped herbs into the olive oil. 'Drip' a little of the olive oil and herb mixture over each pizza.

6. Take some cheese and sprinkle a little on each pizza. Put them under a hot grill until the cheese has melted and the little pizzas are sizzling. That's it. Job done!

HEY BUD ... THAT SURE IS A GREAT FLAVOUR!

Your tongue is covered with little groups of cells called taste buds, which are very sensitive to the flavour of things. The taste buds towards the back of your tongue taste things with a bitter flavour, the ones around the middle of your tongue taste spicy and salty flavours (like those on your mini pizzas) and the ones on the tip of your tongue taste sweet flavours.

Micro Makes